THE BEGINNER'S GUIDE TO ENLIGHTENMENT

BEYOND PERSONALITY

ZUBIN GENIUSTRAINERS

Contents

Epigraph — v

Epigraph — vii

From The Editor's Desk — ix

The Origin — xi

Preface — xiii

1. Introduction To Implicate Technology — 1

2. The Self-help Technology — 2

3. Characteristics Of The Period Prior To The Psychological Stage Of Enlightenment — 3

4. The Time Of Testing — 18

5. Confirmatory Experiences — 19

6. The All-pervasive Influence Of The Emotions — 34

7. Advice On Failure To Attain The Psychological Stage Of Enlightenment — 44

8. Conclusion - The Far Journey — 45

Bibliography — 47

Glossary — 49

Synopsis Of Contents — 51

This Is Everything — 53

EPIGRAPH

Nothing Real Can Be Threatened.

Nothing Unreal Exists.

-A Course In Miracles"

Epigraph

The Real Does Not Die,

The Unreal Never Lived.

-I Am That "

FROM THE EDITOR'S DESK

Though this book was originally published in 1987 I happened to meet with this only in the late 90's through my friend Mr. Mathew who got it from another common friend Gijo. Since there are thousands of books on Enlightenment, I opened the book with my usual skeptic mind; But I was in for a surprise. No Non- sense, No sectorial thoughts, No excusive membership offers, not even the name of the people involved. Age old truth without any paraphernalia.

We made an attempt to meet the wonderful people who took the effort to create this book when my friend Jaise visited UK. But all he could get was a post box number and nothing more. Still we don't know who took the effort to create such a marvelous work.

The original book was not reprinted and currently not in circulation. So we thought of republishing it through Geniustrainers' publication division. And this version is the result of that. We have not made any changes to the content other than adding this intro and two epigraphs and a new cover.

We know this book not meant for all. Yes, Enlightenment or right knowledge is not meant for all. That is the reality. If you are on the path then you will find this book guiding you. If you are not, then this book will not.

May all be liberated
May all be free from suffering
May all be happy

Regards
Zubin Geniustrainers

THE ORIGIN

The Implicate Technology Centre has been formed to meet the extensive and as yet unfulfilled need for self-help books of a secular nature, which explain in clear, direct, everyday terms what enlightenment is and how it can be attained.

Beyond the Personality: the beginner's guide to enlightenment is based on the experience of enlightened individuals living and working as ordinary people in and around London. They have pooled their experience to provide this teaching, so that others can know the benefits of enlightenment.

This book tackles the opportunity created by the current explosion of interest in enlightenment, through the use of secular language and imagery to explore issues which are normally the province of religions.

This teaching of a systematic and coherent secular system of meditation leading to enlightenment, will be completed with the publication of *The advanced guide to enlightenment.* That book is scheduled for publication in late 1987 by The Implicate Technology Centre.

Editor's Note: *The advanced guide to enlightenment* has already published by implicate technologies. Now it is not in print. We will be pblishing the book soon.

PREFACE

The meaning of life is: *life is*.

The fullness of this can only be understood through experiencing the unity that is reality. This understanding through experience is not possible within the terms of your ordinary, day-to-day awareness. The first and most difficult step along the path to understanding is to attain the state of awareness known as the psychological stage of enlightenment.

This state of awareness is accessible to you if you are prepared to commit your whole being, your whole sense of purpose, to the enterprise. This book teaches any ordinary intelligent person how to experience the first or psychological stage of enlightenment within the context of ordinary, day-to-day life. This is the great adventure of the human spirit.

It is your destiny.

The Implicate Technology Centre.

I

Introduction to implicate technology

II

The self-help technology

III

Characteristics of the period prior to the psychological stage of Enlightenment

How do you measure your progress along the path towards the psychological stage of enlightenment?

Reality can be understood either as a mechanical, or as an organic, process - an infinite and a unified whole. Everything that happens within reality has meaning. The first and most difficult step along the path to understanding reality through experience is to grow and expand your awareness until it stabilises in the psychological state known as the first stage of enlightenment.

Reality is an organic machine structured to operate in accordance with immutable laws. To understand and experience reality as it is, your actions must be in harmony with the natural laws which govern and inform all that can be experienced. Each one of us is an integral and organic component of reality.

Reality is an infinite process unfolding through time, configured to operate at one setting only. The past is memory, individual or cultural, the future is both potential and fantasy: always and unendingly the process occurs *now*. As you move towards the psychological stage of enlightenment, through the practice of meditation, progress can be measured by the extent to which you interpret your day-to-day experiences within the context of what is happening now, at this present moment.

Karma is a term used in Eastern implicate technology systems to describe one of the implacable laws of reality. Your karma is the result of the choices you make. In the West, we know karma as the law of cause and effect.

Psychologically, our culture understands this unyielding law as the accumulated weight of experience, preserved within oneself, and shaping one's choices and experiences. The traditional teaching of our deeper psychologies involves a tortuous process of gradually understanding and coming to terms with these deep psychological determinants which shape each individual's behaviour. The teachings offered here show a well-trodden and faster path to freedom from the accumulated weight of experience which shapes each moment experienced in ordinary states of awareness.

As each of us ages and matures, the weight of our burdens increases. In our highly stressful culture, day-to-day life becomes an increasing struggle. Consistent, committed daily practice of this meditation leads to a profoundly fulfilling release from the sense of burden.

The key to releasing the full benefits of meditation lies in understanding the occurrences of your day-to-day life in terms of these teachings. This is the raw beginning of the fundamental process of learning to live your life in meditation. This meditation is a simple self-help tool available to anyone committed to transforming her or his daily experience of living.

The key to effecting the transformation within oneself is very easy to learn, but very hard to apply. The meditation teaches you to focus your concentration on one simple activity. The key is always to understand each moment of each day in terms of these teachings - always to keep the teachings in mind.

To effect the transformation successfully within a hundred days, you need a context within which you can operate meaningfully, to guide you through the many choices you make each day. To attain the psychological stage of enlightenment you need give your allegiance to no force outside yourself. Remember the teachings within the context of <u>Act</u>:

Act according to your intuition

Set face to face with reality, when you are experiencing reality directly, each moment offers you a choice. As you choose or fail to choose, so you create your karma. Follow the still small voice of your intuition.

Don't interfere

Each one of us is an integral and organic component of reality. By interfering, you choose to act against the flow of reality. Allow reality to unfold both within yourself and externally.

Just let things happen

To live in the flow of reality is to experience your life with clarity, serenity and a quiet fulfilling joy. This is the path to integrating your awareness into reality - this is the path to experiencing your life in the fullness of reality. Learn to accept reality as it unfolds.

This teaching on <u>Act</u> is the key to the process of enlightenment, the secret of the golden flower. To live in accordance with these teachings is to experience your life as a dynamically unfolding process. But first you must learn to be passive in the face of reality. Learn actively to accept your ordinary day-to-day reality in its utter fullness.

The measure of how close you are to attaining the psychological stage of enlightenment is the extent to which you are able to understand the experiences of your life in the terms of these teachings while fitting your behaviour within the constructs of <u>Act</u>. As you develop, your intuitive awareness of time will unfold - you will gradually lose the illusory sense of past, present and future; gradually you will gain the ability to live in the ever-present now. Finally, you will be free from the burden of the past, free at last from the psychological burdens which you have carried for so long.

. . . .

<u>Live</u>

Live *the teachings,*
live *the teachings.*

<u>Act</u>

Act *according to your intuition.*
*Don't **interfere**.*
*Just let things **happen**.*

The formula for attaining enlightenment is:

Throughout your life, **<u>Live</u>** and**<u>Act</u>**

. . . .

What is it like to experience life on the path to the psychological stage of enlightenment?

Although each of us is born, lives and dies, the experiences of each life are unique. Similarly, although the mechanics of the path to the first enlightenment are common to all, each of us experiences the path in a different way. In our spiritually barren Western cultures, the path to the psychological enlightenment is challenging, often difficult and sometimes dangerous.

As you develop in understanding, according to your gifts and temperament, so you will seek to articulate the unfolding of reality in the terms of your worldview. You may choose to articulate your experience in the religious terms of mainstream Christianity, Judaism or Islam; or you may be inclined towards the spiritual models of the Jewish Kabbala, Islamic Sufism, Western Paganism or the higher teachings of Hinduism, Buddhism or Taoism. Equally, in our largely secular Western cultures, you may be an atheist or an agnostic.

Your belief structure determines how you understand and articulate your experience of reality. All belief structures act as a distorting mechanism on the clear understanding and experiencing of reality. This teaching of the clear setting face to face with reality offers knowledge based on experience. No belief structure is required - simply practice the teachings.

Even the atheist and agnostic have belief structures, we all do. Learn to be guided not by beliefs, but by what you know and understand through direct experience. Your beliefs are an impediment on the path to understanding; what matters is that you directly experience reality.

As you experience reality directly, you will seek to articulate your understanding in the terms of a belief structure relevant to your needs. You can choose with equal validity to follow a religious or a secular path. All models of reality reflect reality according to the varying needs of the cultures, times and individuals which produce and utilise them.

Although all models of reality are valid in different ways and in different cultural environments, do not expect to find that the representatives of these models are trained to understand and deal with the issues raised in this book. Priests, ministers and rabbis are ordinary individuals trained in theological and religious matters. Their training does not, in general, provide them with a path towards understanding reality through experience.

As you experience the difficulties of the continuous emotional transformations necessarily involved, you may be tempted to turn to the medical profession for guidance and assistance during this period of uncertainty in your life. Be extremely cautious in approaching a profession which is trained to understand and treat the human body as separate parts. These people are unlikely to be trained in the skills of treating a person experiencing the transformations leading to wholeness.

Become aware of the alternative therapies available. Many of these involve inexpensive treatment of the whole person. As you become sensitive to your own needs, you will be drawn to an appropriate source of healing.

In the spiritually advanced cultures of the East, it is traditional to be taught this process of the gradual transformation of awareness directly by a living, recognised master. Our Western cultures have developed on the sound basis of the Judeo-Christian code of ethics. In the current spiritually barren cultural conditions, it is unlikely that you will be taught in the traditional face to face manner by a living teacher. In general, you will have to develop, through practice of the skills taught in this book, the ability to survive, flower and transform, in a culture which is inimical and hostile to the process of inner development.

Finally, do not anticipate understanding or help from your family or friends. It is possible that through their lack of understanding of the process you are experiencing they will react with incomprehension, hostility and fear. Through practice of the day-to-day adaptation and survival skills taught in chapter 8, you will, in time, find the living guidance, support and companionship you truly need and deserve.

• • • •

How does one experience the uncertainty of being set face to face with reality?

As you develop in understanding, through the experience of integrating the fruits of meditation into your everyday life, you enter into a period of increasing uncertainty. Your previously held beliefs about what is important and real crumble in the face of direct experience of reality. However disconcerting, unpleasant and miserable you find this experience, remember it is a necessary and healing part of the process of becoming set face to face with reality.

This state of uncertainty is a necessary process of eroding and dismantling, through your reaction to the circumstances of your life, the belief structures underpinning your personality. The structures you have imposed on reality, the way your beliefs have shaped your thoughts and actions, are being dissolved in the face of reality. Reality devours the personality.

This process heals through removal of the illusory limitations of the personality. This natural, painful and difficult experience leads to your awareness stabilising, in time, beyond the personality. It is only when one's awareness operates outside of emotional and intellectual structures that the true setting face to face with reality can begin.

The feelings of misery and sorrow which occur now are the birth pangs of your new awareness. Like natural childbirth, the experience becomes more fulfilling when one learns to detach oneself from the pain. Gradually, as you endure through time, you will experience a new understanding, a release from pain into clarity, serenity and quiet joyousness.

The uncertainty of this period, as the illusory structures of the personality are swept away, leads to a profound sense of instability. The difficulties and dangers of this stage can be compounded if those with whom one is accustomed to share one's life are unaware of, or hostile to, the process of inner transformation. The way to emerge from these difficulties in your life is to <u>Live</u> and <u>Act</u>.

If you seek to interfere, in your distress, you will only gain more trouble. Learn to accept without interference the events of your life as they unfold. Above all, learn to develop your sense of empowering your life only by following your intuition.

At this time, your life as you have understood and experienced it will seem to be dissolving in uncertainty. Learn not to seek to impose your own sense of order on reality. Put aside your desire for stability and security in your life.

Through daily practice of the meditation in the context given, you will gradually develop a profound sense of inner stillness and security. Gradually, you will learn to accept the conditions of your life without interfering. Above all, learn to shape your life actively, in accordance with the natural laws governing reality, by becoming centred in the midst of conditions.

Throughout your life, <u>Live</u> and <u>Act</u>. There are no circumstances or conditions, no hazards of life, which cannot be harmoniously negotiated through practice of these skills. Rise above the circumstances of your life through becoming centred in the midst of conditions.

. . . .

What does it mean, to be centred in the midst of conditions?

This is a very fine phrase: centred in the midst of conditions. It should be thought about carefully. When you understand this as a continuous experience, and not just intellectually or emotionally, you will have attained the psychological stage of enlightenment.

The conditions which constrain our lives are common to each of us, but the specific details vary according to individual circumstances. These conditions are imposed both internally within the personality, and externally upon the personality. They operate on both the material and non-material levels of reality.

There are ten conditions which interweave, waxing and waning endlessly, to form each moment you experience. The circumstances of your life are shaped by these conditions: karma; space and time; physical, emotional and intellectual limiting factors; moral and social constraints, and political and economic pressures. The purpose of the power discipline taught later in this chapter is to empower you to deal effectively with and to transform the conditions of your life.

The condition of karma is discussed in detailed contemporary terms in chapter 4. In our spiritually barren, late-twentieth-century Western cultures, we have only a slight degree of understanding of the crucially important nature of karma. Unless you are responsive to the promptings of karma in your life, you can have no hope or prospect of a genuinely fulfilling life.

Birth and death punctuate our lives. As we age, our lives unfold through understanding and experience. Time is the medium through which all things occur.

Each of our bodies requires space to exist. The things which exist through space constrain and limit us, through our needs and desires for them. Space is the medium through which all things occur.

Time and space are inextricably woven together. They are the basic conditions of existence. Every being with any form of awareness, and every thing, is subject to these dual forces.

The conditions of space and time are discussed more fully in the transpersonal meditations of chapter 5. The full teachings on the nature of space and time are beyond the scope of this book. The final stage of enlightenment, the union of self with reality, only occurs when the unified nature of space and time has been fully realised through experience.

In our cultures, we are familiar with discussing and analysing our lives in terms of the seven remaining conditions. This chapter discusses them within the context of Implicate Technology disciplines. Practice of these disciplines will empower you to understand and break free from the oppressive forces dominating your life.

Be clear: every unenlightened person lives a life hemmed in and limited by the ten conditions - just because you are unaware of your own limitations doesn't mean that they don't exist. The purpose of these teachings is to provide you with the skills to triumph over the conditions of your life. If you confuse this with vain dreams of triumph over your opponents, then reality, through the workings of karma, will deal with such unenlightened behaviour in its own way.

In the midst of these conditions is yourself, experiencing life through action and reaction to things and people. Through practice of these teachings you will learn to focus your awareness of reality through the still, calm centre of your self. This is what it means to be 'centred in the midst of conditions'.

. . . .

In what way are emotions, experienced within the limitations of the personality, relatively illusory?

Prior to attaining the first stage of enlightenment, the emotions are the primary medium through which you experience the conditions of life. You respond across the range of emotions according to the way your personality interacts with reality. As the circumstances of your life unfold, so you respond emotionally to a greater or lesser degree, according to your individual nature.

It is possible for a personality to appear to operate primarily from an intellectual rather than an emotional base. This is simply a form of emotional camouflage, based on a flight from the reality of emotional experience. It is not possible to experience life fully through the intellect.

All aspects of the personality set limiting structures on the direct experiencing of reality. The emotional range of responses, as experienced within the constructs of the personality, embodies a relatively underdeveloped reaction to reality. In relation to one who experiences reality from the standpoint of the first stage of enlightenment, these emotional responses are best understood as self-generated, self-perpetuating activities, illusory in the face of reality.

The experience of time as fragmented into past, present and future becomes understood as an illusion relative to the sense of the eternal present which is experienced after attaining the first stage of enlightenment. In the same way, the emotions experienced as real within the limitations of the personality become experienced as only relatively real. After the first stage of enlightenment, emotions are still experienced within the personality, but now such emotions are understood as being of only relative and limited importance in the face of reality.

. . . .

How is one to deal with the experience of life in the midst of these conditions?

One's reaction at first, before practice of these teachings has borne fruit, remains as before. One acts and reacts according to the blend of emotions and the system of values held, which form the basis for the choices made by the personality at each moment. One incurs karmic consequences within the relatively illusory limitations of the personality.

As your experience of these teachings develops, you will learn new skills through the practice of meditation. At first, you will simply develop basic skills such as control of the breathing and patience. These are very valuable skills in themselves; a great deal depends on them.

It makes no difference to the realisation of the fruits of these teachings in your life whether you are unemployed or in work, poor or not. In the path to enlightenment, the absence of money no more hinders one who lacks it than its presence helps one who possesses it. All are equal in the face of reality.

As you progress in your commitment to the daily practice of meditation, the practice itself will become the central thread of your life. For this, you depend totally on yourself, you need no objects and only the simplest of conditions. This is something for yourself and completely within your own power to achieve.

You may object that not everyone can ensure time alone and uninterrupted - it is not always easy. The answer is that if you cannot create such simple conditions then there will be no enlightenment. This is very hard work, according to your life circumstances.

Once awoken, the drive towards enlightenment is strong within us. Everything else pales into unimportance beside it; yet the path to enlightenment involves all we experience. Practice of these teachings will awaken your innate capacity to experience enlightenment.

Gradually, as the fruits of meditation ripen in your life, you will begin to experience the events and activities of each day with a new understanding. As your awareness goes through the many emotional transformations before the first enlightenment, you will gradually develop the ability to understand reality in a simple, clear and direct way. In the midst of conditions, you will be better able to understand, and deal with, the power structures imposed on your life.

. . . .

What are these power structures which influence each life so deeply?

Each one, each thing, in existence is subject to the conditions of time and space. We each, sooner or later, will experience death. We each have similar minimum requirements for physical survival.

To live our lives, we each require an adequate supply of food, drink, shelter and warmth. One way or another, we each must find a means to procure what we need and desire. In this way we are all the same.

We place a great deal of value on what we need and desire, whether people or things, explicate or implicate, experienced physically, emotionally, intellectually or beyond. Through our individual circumstances and conditions, these needs and desires shape our lives. To fulfil them, we learn to acquire, and submit to, power.

These skills in the ways of power are developed from birth, with the first demands for fulfilment. As we grow to adulthood, we learn to deal with the power structures surrounding those involved in our lives. We each, according to our willingness to understand, learn from experience who holds the power in any situation.

This holds true for all of us. All things are created through power. The more clearly you are aware how power is structured in a particular situation, the more likely you are to create a satisfying outcome.

In the final analysis, we each create the shape of our own lives, subject to the explicate and implicate laws of reality. According to the clarity of your mind, you will be more or less aware of the truth of this. Understanding your life in the context of these teachings will empower you to achieve a more fulfilling life through practice of the power discipline.

. . . .

What is this power discipline?

It is a way of acting, through understanding, to negotiate your way through the hazards of any particular situation. In every situation, in every set of conditions, no matter how adverse, there is always power available to you. Committed practice of the power discipline will enable you to identify and utilise the power inherent in any situation.

Preparation for the power discipline begins with daily practice of the meditation. Gradually, you will learn to incorporate the fruits of meditation into your life by <u>Live</u>-ing and <u>Act</u>-ing. In this way you learn to set yourself face to face with reality.

The more directly you are set face to face with reality, the more you see any situation clearly, as it is, the more possible it is to produce a fulfilling outcome. The power discipline reflects the harmonious laws governing reality. To use power for unselfish ends incurs positive karmic consequences, to use power for selfish ends incurs negative karmic consequences.

The law of karma will be discussed more fully in chapter 4. It is inviolable. It is inherent in the structure of reality.

Practice of this discipline will empower you to deal with any situation, through a clear understanding. As you choose, through your actions, so you shape your life. According to your motives, so you will incur the karmic consequences of your actions.

You are free to choose and to <u>Act</u>, now, and at all times, as best you are able in the prevailing circumstances. We are all subject to the conditions of space, time and karma. Within this context, we each must face reality.

Practice of the power discipline will help you face reality. You are free to use it unselfishly or selfishly, for good or evil, according to your nature. The power discipline is a smooth, flowing, harmonious, organic action, understood in three steps:

<u>Input</u>, <u>Pivot</u>then<u>Act</u>

. . . .

How does the <u>Input</u> step unfold?

The first step is the one in which the intellect is very important. Your intellect is an essential tool to help you understand reality through analysis. Remember, however, intellectual analysis is, in itself, inadequate to the task of understanding reality through experience.

You begin by becoming aware of the situation you are in. Every situation occurs within many overlapping sets of conditions. The more conditions you are aware of, the wider the context within which you understand the situation, the better you are able to deal directly with reality.

Begin with the simplest conditions. Become aware of how the power is structured and who wields it. Begin to face reality directly.

Become aware of the physical, emotional, intellectual, moral, social, political and economic conditions determining the outcome of each situation you find yourself in. All of this occurs within the context of space, time and karma. We each live our lives, as best we can, within the circumstances imposed on us by these conditions.

Begin by understanding each situation within the terms of the lessons you have learnt by the daily practice of meditation. Become aware of who holds the power and how it is wielded. Learn to identify and use your own power, and when to submit to another's.

The power analysis of the physical situation embraces all the significant physical elements. These objects, people or forces empower yourself and others in myriad ways, through legal, moral, or physical ownership. Learn to identify the nature of the power involved, who holds the power and how it is wielded. Only then will you have a clear understanding of how you stand in relation to this power.

The power analysis of the emotional situation embraces all the discernable and relevant emotions of yourself and others. These emotions arise through the complex of our needs and desires, for people and things. The more you are able to rise above the emotions of your personality, through realising their relatively illusory nature, the less will you be subject both to the power of your emotions and to other people's capacity to wield power over you through your emotional links with them or with things.

The power analysis of the intellectual situation embraces all the aspects of the experience which are susceptible to intellectual discrimination. The function of your intellect is to assist in understanding your experience, it is secondary to experience itself. The ideas of the mind are relevant to us relative to our ability to use them to attain what we need and desire.

The power analysis of the moral environment embraces all those activities and desires, concerning people and things, which operate within your own or others' moral constructs. All moral codes have power in a particular situation, according to the extent to which those present subscribe to the code. Become aware of the effects of moral conditions on your own viewpoint and that of others.

The power analysis of the social situation embraces all the frameworks of custom and law which constrain our behaviour. The power of these frameworks, in any specific situation, depends on how enforceable they are in subtle and overt ways. Become aware of the social constraints imposed on and by yourself and others.

The power analysis of the political situation embraces all the ways employed by yourself and others to gain your own ends. Politics, in the widest sense, is the process whereby individuals and groups control and manipulate, to impose their will upon others. Learn to recognise who is doing what, to whom, and why - then you will understand the politics of the situation.

The power analysis of the economic situation embraces all the conditions imposed on us by our own and others' needs and desires for material things. Control of material things is usually maintained by physical force, or through more subtle means. In any situation, learn to recognise how you are constrained by your needs and desires for material things.

These conditions interweave and combine, to a greater or lesser degree, in each situation you face. Through practice of the <u>Input</u> step, you will become aware of the conditions imposed on yourself and others. Be clear in your understanding of your constraints; set yourself face to face with reality.

The complexity of this process of analysis reflects the complexity of your actual experience. As you first practise, <u>Input</u> may be time-consuming and require a great deal of thought about your life circumstances. After a time, as you become more aware, you will be able to perform the <u>Input</u> step with speed and fluidity.

. . . .

How does the <u>Pivot</u> step unfold?

The <u>Input</u> step, the process of analysis, is as complete as you are willing and able to make it. You become aware, to a greater or lesser degree according to the amount and quality of your effort, of the conditions imposed on yourself and others. You are aware of the way the power in the situation is structured.

The task of the <u>Pivot</u> step is to prepare for an action which will alter the balance of power, harmoniously. For an action to achieve this, it must be simple, daring and effective. Such an action can only be supplied by your intuition.

The process of analysis, through the <u>Input</u> step, reveals to you the configuration of conditions which shapes the environment under analysis. You are now aware of the forces, pressures and people who hold, or are subject to, power in the situation. Before you can harmoniously weave a path through all these conditions you must become still.

Be centred in the midst of conditions. Understand that your personal configuration of needs and desires is illusory relative to the implacable power structures of reality. Be still, simply understand the situation as it is, and not from the relatively illusory and selfish viewpoint of your personality.

As you become centred in the midst of conditions, your thoughts will become calm, still and clear. You will cease to understand things in terms of the satisfaction of your needs and desires. You will understand that if you act to further your personal desires, reality will devour your works - none is exempt from this process.

Poised, centred in the midst of conditions, your understanding of the situation will configure in a lightning flash of intuition. Aware of when to wield and to yield to power, your intuition will articulate your next action. This is the moment when it becomes possible to <u>Pivot</u> the balance of power.

. . . .

How does the <u>Act</u> step unfold?

There are ten conditions, not nine. There are ten conditions, not eleven. Every situation you are set face to face with, in reality, can be understood as configured in the terms of these ten conditions - karma; space and time; physical, emotional and intellectual limiting factors; moral and social constraints, political and economic pressures.

The **Input** step, the analysis of the situation, is completed. The **Pivot** step, the lightning flash of intuitive understanding creating the possibility of harmoniously transforming the balance of power, is completed. Now is the time to **<u>Act</u>**.

The <u>Act</u>ion you take should flow harmoniously from your circumstances. Through understanding your experience, your intuition will guide you towards the next step. Learn to act on the still, quiet, voice of your intuition.

For your **<u>Act</u>**ion to avoid incurring negative karmic consequences, it should not interfere with people or things. To interfere is an act of self-will and goes against the flow of reality. Reality is a harmonious, self-balancing, unity; if you act against the natural flow of events you will, sooner or later, incur a corresponding negative reaction.

When you**<u>Act</u>**, just let things happen, easily and naturally, within yourself and in terms of your behaviour towards other people and things. In every situation, no matter how apparently hopeless, there is always power for you to use harmoniously. If you wield and yield to power in an organic, flowing way, reality will unfold in its own manner.

. . . .

IV
The Time of Testing

V
Confirmatory Experiences

How is this chapter to be used?

This chapter can usefully be read by anyone. Unlike the remainder of the book, it is written exclusively from the transpersonal point of view. Accordingly, what is described in this chapter will only be fully realisable by those who have attained the first stage of enlightenment.

| | | | | | | | | | | |

Welcome, and congratulations. You have struggled long and hard, requiring all your courage and powers of endurance to overcome your fears and difficulties. Now is the time to rest and take stock of your new and growing awareness of reality.

You have successfully completed the first and most difficult step along the path to understanding the unity of reality through experience. Become aware of and enjoy your newfound freedom. By now, you know as a certainty that there are such things as enlightenment, and a path, and that you are firmly set on that path.

Do not be proud of your achievement: instead, become aware of the wonder of reality as it unfolds to your inner vision. Learn not to be self-seeking in the face of reality: realise that it is not 'I' who lives, but 'that' which lives you. Care for others: as you travel along the path you will realise that we are all indissolubly linked in the face of reality; no-one in existence is exempt from karma.

You have struggled much, endured much, understood much. Yet, for all that, your work has only begun. You are now correctly positioned to understand, through your own experience, the nature and purpose of reality.

Remember, the way ahead is long and hard. In terms of emotional suffering the searing pains and tensions of the time of testing will grow dim as your capacity to operate free from intellectual and emotional constraints grows bright. Just as your present awareness completely transcends the limitations of what was your ordinary, everyday awareness, so, too, does the awareness brought about by the final stage of enlightenment transform and transcend your present limitations.

The worst is past, yet the hardest challenge lies ahead. This apparent contradiction is resolved by developing your latent abilities and powers; these will develop spontaneously to assist you as you travel along the path. All that counts, in reality, is where you are along the path in relation to the final stage of enlightenment: between the first and last stages of enlightenment are many transformations of consciousness, but all that matters at any one time is the next step along the path to the final stage of enlightenment.

What, then, is the final stage of enlightenment? The logical conclusion of this teaching of the clear setting face to face with reality must be that the final stage of enlightenment is to realise the unconditioned state; but it is not only for yourself that this is to be done. Full, absolute and final enlightenment is only realised when compassion for the unenlightened is awoken - regardless of the outer form of that life, the fully enlightened person is dedicated, through unremitting inner perseverance, to assisting all others to realise the unconditioned state.

The uses of this chapter are twofold. Firstly, practice of the meditation technique taught here will assist you to stabilise your new awareness, to settle firmly in the psychological stage of enlightenment. Secondly, continued practice in meditation, as directed, will prepare you for the full teaching contained in chapter 2 of the follow-up work from the Implicate Technology Centre, *The advanced guide to enlightenment.* That chapter teaches how to integrate a life based on meditation into your social, moral, economic and political environment.

. . . .

What are the differences between the first stage of enlightenment and an awareness based on a gradual integration into, and involvement with, your wider cultural environment?

The primary function of this book is to provide a simple self-help technology which, with committed daily use, leads to the first significant transformation in consciousness. The technology leading to the full understanding of reality through experience is beyond the scope of this book. The secondary function of this book is to enhance the implicate technology skills developed to attain the first stage of enlightenment, so that you will be able to set your life in harmony with the wider cultural forces shaping your environment: the moral, social, economic and political conditions.

To achieve this, one needs both a model of reality and an understanding of the true nature of meditation. The model of reality serves as a goal; only when the accuracy and completeness of the model is realised is the final stage of enlightenment attained. Meditation is the priceless, free tool available to each of us to assist us in the transforming and transcending of the conditions of our lives.

The model of reality is this: the true nature of reality is consciousness without content, which none the less permits all contents to exist. This cannot be understood within the range of experiences accessible to a person with a normal level of consciousness. A person who has attained the first stage of enlightenment is correctly positioned at the start of the path which leads towards understanding the fullness and unity of reality through experience.

The experience you are aiming for is to understand what is meant by a consciousness without content. To be able to experience this, you must develop your understanding through further committed daily practice of meditation. The true purpose of meditation is to develop your ability to still the process of thinking.

To still the thinking, to transcend the thought process, is a skill which you will develop, quite naturally and spontaneously, through meditation. As your everyday experience unfolds, you will gradually realise that your experience up to attaining the first stage of enlightenment has completely misled you as to the nature of reality. The goal of the culturally integrated and committed level of awareness, as discussed extensively in chapter 2 of *The advanced guide to enlightenment,* is to understand, with an intuitive certainty of knowledge, the true nature of reality; keep in mind, though, that this is not yet direct experience of the true nature of reality.

. . . .

What is the meditation on serenity and harmony?

There are many, many possible confirmatory experiences to be had after attaining the first stage of enlightenment, which may seem strange, simple, wonderful, even frightening. What you will experience will be a function of your own nature and individual gifts. Remember, everything you experience is karmically configured to lead you towards understanding your own nature.

To realise that a thing is so is to confirm it through experience. As this phase of the meditation unfolds, you will have many experiences which are real to you, but very difficult to articulate to others. The reason for this is that they are too simple to be expressed in words. Yet they are profoundly satisfying to experience.

To practice any of the meditations taught in this chapter you need to make one slight and difficult change in your daily meditation. Count the breaths and think only of the subject of your meditation; cut off all other trains of thought or fantasies. Remember, the goal is attained by living in meditation.

After the first stage of enlightenment, as your experience in meditation unfolds, the practice of counting the breaths may become an irrelevant distraction for you. Provided you are able to concentrate your thoughts on the subject of your meditation, there is no harm in gradually dropping the practice of counting breaths. The purpose of all meditative practices is to develop the ability to concentrate your attention on one thing at a time.

The aim of the meditation on serenity and harmony is to analyse your current condition. Become aware of your detachment, its benefits and how you arrive at this inner calm. Above all, learn how to sustain it for longer and longer periods.

The key to a full unfolding of your awareness, in the face of reality, lies in expanding your capacity to experience serenity and harmony in the midst of conditions. By attaining the first stage of enlightenment, you have broken free of the emotional and intellectual conditions constraining your personality. You will rapidly learn through experience that you have to work hard to sustain your new detachment - some days are warmer, some days are cooler.

Serenity is based on the capacity to remain detached from emotional conditions. You will still experience your own emotions and those of others; only, now, you need no longer be driven by these forces. Through serenity, you can transcend your habitual emotional behaviour patterns.

With practice at this meditation you will become increasingly free to choose your response to each set of conditions you experience. To operate in harmony, simply <u>Live</u> and <u>Act</u> throughout your life. Your karmic task is to benefit yourself and others through your actions.

Do not think that because you can sustain this state of serenity and harmony, you possess any inherent or acquired superiority over others. In reality, there is only one path for us all, and you are simply further along that path than others. You convey your understanding of these teachings primarily through your behaviour. Words are secondary to this.

. . . .

What is the meditation on the model of reality?

The root Implicate Technology image of reality is: consciousness without content, which none the less permits all contents to exist. The truth of this is all-embracing. The function of this meditation is limited to preparing your understanding only; the meditations leading to experience of the final stage of enlightenment will be included in the follow-up teaching from the Implicate Technology Centre on the nature and purpose of reality: *The advanced guide to enlightenment.*

The nature of your mind reflects the nature of reality: your mind is a microcosm of reality. The first stage of the process leading to a fully unfolded experience of reality is to develop an understanding of your mind. When you have understood the structure and functioning of your mind, you will then be in a position to experience the inherent unity and fullness of reality.

The function of meditation, when sustained with committed effort over time, is to produce a still mind. Put simply, this is the mind in its natural state, fully aware and freed from the tyranny of the thought process. You need give no thought at this stage to this process of developing a still mind; it will occur quite naturally as you develop your work in meditation, as taught in this chapter and chapter 2 of *The advanced guide to enlightenment.*

The mind, when uninhibited by the process of having thoughts, perceives clearly that the true experience of reality is of existence unfolding spontaneously, according to the inherent implicate laws. A measure of your progress towards advanced meditation is the development of the capacity to experience your life as unfolding naturally and spontaneously. Be clear: any thought or action, occurring outside of <u>Act</u>'s guidelines, acts against the flow of reality and incurs negative karmic consequences, whose nature will be according to the true needs of your nature.

Through sustained, committed meditation, the thought-process slows gradually and imperceptibly. The richest fruits of meditation can only be realised once one understands, through experience, that the true nature of mind is emptiness and silence. A measure of your progress towards the advanced meditative practices is to be found in the relative decrease in the pace of the thoughts; when you experience thoughts as unfolding interminably and endlessly, but more slowly this week than last week, then you are progressing in meditation.

A mind which has attained emptiness and silence is far more aware and more powerful than a mind operating at the level of normal consciousness or the first stage of enlightenment. Such a mind is aware of its contents and is no longer preoccupied with compulsive satisfaction of needs and desires. The world, as rich and beautiful as ever in its fullness, still unfolds moment by moment, but it no longer dominates consciousness.

When the fullness of the world ceases to press on consciousness, then the mind turns naturally towards understanding the nature and purpose of reality. Before you can fully understand reality through experience, you must understand the nature of your own mind. You must first understand that the thoughts in your mind create your experience of reality.

From your own attainment of the psychological stage of enlightenment, you will be aware how the experience of emotional conditions is significantly determined by one's unconscious emotional projections. The emotions you were unaware of, before the first stage of enlightenment, none the less deeply shaped the experiences of your life. Changes in your feelings produced corresponding changes in your conception of the external world.

From your current, relatively enlightened, perspective, you now can understand that the emotional conditions experienced are relatively illusory, because they are the externalised products of mind. There is a general principle embodied here which is equally applicable to all conditions. Meditate on this long and hard; when you have developed an intuitive understanding of this principle, you will be clearly set on the path to advanced meditation.

. . . .

What is the meditation on the unity of time?

To ordinary consciousness, time is experienced as yesterday, today and tomorrow. Yesterday is the subject of individual memory and cultural history; tomorrow is the subject of individual and cultural fears and hopes. Ordinary consciousness is rarely located in today, here and now.

Our cultural habits reinforce and reflect this fragmented view, which is a product of the unenlightened mind. This individual and cultural fragmentation of time into the separate elements of past, present and future is real to the unenlightened, but relatively illusory to those who have attained the first stage of enlightenment. In reality, past, present and future function as a unified force.

The purpose of this meditation is to help you realise the unity of time. Practice in this meditation will develop your intuitive understanding of the unity of past, present and future in each set of circumstances you experience now. Understanding the true nature of time, through experience, is within the grasp of anyone who has broken free of the emotional and intellectual personality limitations; that is to say, one who has attained the first stage of enlightenment is in a position to understand that reality always, and only, unfolds now.

The illusion of the past being separate from the present is broken through realising that all of your past, increasingly distilled and refined in meaning as you progress along the path, is retained in your mind. The past is never settled in the relatively enlightened mind; its meaning and significance are continuously being understood in new and wider contexts, as awareness unfolds in the face of reality. Karma is the link incorporating the past into the present: what occurs now, spontaneously, is the karmic outcome of your previous choices.

The illusion of the future being separate from the present is broken through realising that the future, in its full potential, is inherent in seed form in the present moment. To the relatively enlightened mind, the future is beheld as unfolding from the potential of the present; its potential meaning and significance is continuously understood in new and wider contexts. Karma is the link incorporating the future into the present: what will occur, spontaneously, will be the outcome of present thoughts and actions.

The present, incorporating past and future, unfolds spontaneously and uncontrollably, according to the implicate laws inherent in conditioned existence. To the relatively enlightened person, awareness unfolds spontaneously, ever spiralling outwards in the face of reality. Each moment is understood and experienced simply and directly, on its own terms.

Meditate long and hard on the unity of time. Time is one of the key conditions you must understand, through experience, before you can attain the final stage of enlightenment. Once you have mastered this meditation you are in a position to understand the true nature of time: which is that you, your thoughts and all of conditioned existence, unfold, now, in the face of consciousness.

· · · ·

What is the meditation on hearing?

Not all of the confirmatory experiences can be expressed in words; reality is too simple and unified for words. What you will experience is a function of your own nature and karma. If you accept these experiences as real, then they are real to you.

The purpose of these confirmatory experiences is to help you to understand the links between your own nature and reality. As you will gradually learn, the experiencing of reality solely through the five senses is limited and relatively illusory compared to the experiencing of the enlightened state. This meditation on hearing is an illustration of the general principle that reality is not structured, and does not function, in a way that is comprehensible within the limitations of sight, hearing, smell, taste and touch.

Reality only becomes comprehensible when one activates one's sixth sense of direct intuitive perception. Committed daily practice of meditation develops your sixth sense. As your intuitive perception of reality unfolds, you will experience a subtle, but real and lasting, change in your sense of hearing.

As the meditation takes holds and produces fruit, one's way of hearing alters, naturally and spontaneously. One becomes aware of hearing the ordinary sounds of the environment in a different way. One experiences sounds in this way: each is heard quite clearly, quite separately, and each is equally significant in your hearing. Through meditation on this experience, one comes to realise how constrained is the hearing of normal consciousness. The lesson of this meditation is simple. Life is: become aware.

. . . .

What is the meditation on sexual energy?

To progress along the path to advanced meditation, to realise the meaning and purpose of existence requires a source of energy to power the final, massive transformation of consciousness. The teachings of this book, when fully realised, will guide you in your work with karma, and prepare you for the advanced meditations on the meaning and purpose of existence. This meditation, which requires much hard work to master, will prepare your whole being for the full experiencing of the unity of reality.

All models of reality take a stance on the role of sexuality in life. The Judeo-Christian tradition advocates confining sexual activity within a religiously sanctified, heterosexual marriage. Many religious models of reality advocate renouncing sexual activity altogether and re-channelling the sexual energy through chastity, via a life as a priest, nun or monk.

Most models of reality take a moral attitude towards sexual activity, allowing this and barring that. The Implicate Technology secular model of reality relies for its morality on the inherent moral patterning of existence, as imposed on all human beings by karma. Provided sexual activity is in harmony with the guidelines of <u>Act</u>, it matters not whether the activity is bisexual, homosexual or heterosexual, occurring inside or outside of marriage - all other constraints are not natural, being merely the products of moral, social, political and economic conditions.

From the secular point of view of Implicate Technology, all aspects of existence are understood as being, in practice, illusorily separate strands of an organically unified and purposive whole. In the face of reality, provided your sexual activity is in accordance with <u>Act</u>, your choice of partners and lifestyles is, simply, part of the raw material of your life, which you can refine through understanding into the experience of enlightenment. The primary issue, if you are to attain the final stage of enlightenment, through this or any other teaching, is not how conventional morality views your sexual orientation, but the correct use of your sexual energy.

It is not the purpose of this particular meditation to teach you the specific techniques of using the body's natural power source to attain the final stage of enlightenment. The scope of this meditation is confined to making you aware of the nature and functioning of your sexual energy, and to making a significant start on generating and utilising your body's implicate power source. The true nature and purpose of existence can only be realised through a form of implicate technology: sexual energy is the prime psycho-physiological link between your consciousness and the implicate nature of reality.

Be clear on this: your own sexual energy, stored within your body and properly used, in accordance with natural implicate laws, is the power source for the transformation of your consciousness. Through retaining, understanding and mastering your sexual energy, you attain full, final and absolute enlightenment. Through wasting your energy in unenlightened sexual activity, you will abuse the most precious gift your body produces for you.

The practice of this meditation is very simple to undertake, but very hard to sustain. It matters not if you fail, especially in the early stages - simply begin the meditation again. What is important is to develop an unwavering determination to succeed: temporary, even repeated, failure is less important than developing a singleness of mind to succeed.

The first step is to retain the sexual energy your body generates. If you are a man, this means retaining semen through avoiding ejaculation. If you are a woman, this means avoiding the release of sexual energy when menstruating. The remainder of this chapter is written from the viewpoint of male sexual energy.

Practice of this meditation does not preclude any form of sexual activity, provided it is in accord with <u>Act</u>. The meditation may also be practised during periods of celibacy or by renouncing sexual activity through chastity, provided such activities occur within the guidelines of <u>Act</u>. The key lies in retaining your sexual energy, not in the nature of your sexual activity.

Sexual activity involving this meditation can occur on your own through masturbation, or with a partner or partners. The practice in each case is the same: learn to refrain from physiologically-based orgasm. As you develop in this practice, through repeated failure then gradual success, you will begin to understand, slowly and naturally, the power inherent in your psycho-physiological system.

The practice of this meditation is the same for a person who does not experience orgasms. Your body's adaptive powers will compensate in a natural way. The essence of the technique lies in transmuting retained sexual energy.

The goal is not complete abstention from physiological orgasm. A fair but demanding target to set yourself is thirty days between orgasms. Be clear: this need not mean thirty days between sexual activities; that is a function of personal choice and the circumstances of your life.

Do not delude yourself that physiological orgasm is a great pleasure and release which you cannot do without. You only think this because you have nothing to compare such orgasms with. Be assured: the pleasures you will experience, on many levels of your being, will transcend, in intensity and power, anything unenlightened sexual activity can offer.

The actual techniques you use to refrain from physiological orgasm are a matter of personal experience and choice, subject to <u>Act</u>. There are many books offering sound advice for men on delaying ejaculation; there are very few for women on avoiding the release of sexual energy when menstruating. Our culture promotes achieving orgasm for both men and women: as you develop in this meditation, you will come to understand, through personal experience, that the key sexual activity is to practise retaining the sexual energy naturally and spontaneously produced by your body.

The key to realising this control is to understand, through meditation, that a physiologically-based orgasm is triggered by mental activity. As you learn to control your mind, you will learn to control your orgasms. All physically-based control techniques are inferior to this level of mental control.

The second step, in this yoga of sexual energy, is to understand through experience the energy which is retained in your body by the practice of not having physiological orgasm. After sexual activity which does not release the body's natural energy through physiological orgasm, there remains considerable tension in your psycho-physiological system. This tension can express itself in a range of symptoms, from simple muscular tension to thoughts whirling endlessly round until you think your head will burst.

The goal of this stage of the meditation is to attain control of the retained sexual energy so as to integrate it into your whole psycho-physiological system, your whole, conditioned, being. You gain nothing by attempting to rush this process or by blaming yourself for failure. What you are trying to develop, above all else, is the unwavering determination to succeed in this meditation.

Your position at the beginning of the second step in this meditation is simple. You have engaged in sexual activity on one or more occasions, alone or accompanied, and through the habit of your body, or effort and practised determination, you have refrained from the release of physiological orgasm. Sooner or later, you will need or desire the release of orgasm to free you from the tensions sweeping your body and your mind.

It is this need or desire for the release of orgasm which you will now learn to transcend. Be patient and meditate long and hard. As you develop mastery, over a sustained period of committed practice, you will learn to experience pleasure in entirely new and satisfying ways.

The method of releasing yourself from the tensions sweeping your body and mind is twofold. Firstly, at any time, enter into the deep, slow breathing you have become accustomed to from your meditation practice. Secondly, learn to raise your retained energy from the sexual energy centre in your groin to the highest energy centre at the crown of your head.

Begin with a transition, willed or spontaneous, to deep, slow, meditative breathing. Do this during sexual activity, while working, while just relaxing at home or in any circumstances you can. The meditative breathing will help you to become centred in the midst of conditions.

This is a process you learn to achieve by experience. There are virtually no sets of conditions during which meditative breathing cannot be entered into. You must be your own teacher in this matter.

Now, with greater or lesser ease, you have settled into meditative breathing. Your psycho-physiological organism, your mind and body, is in a state of tension. You need or desire the release of orgasm.

The source of this disturbance in your whole organism is the sexual energy you have retained through not experiencing the pleasure and release of physiological orgasm. This energy, naturally produced every day by your body, and retained either by your body's natural functioning or by an act of experienced will, is located, at first, in the sexual energy centre. Your task now is to raise this energy to the crown energy centre: by first achieving, then sustaining, this practice, you generate all the power you will need to transform your experience of reality.

From your experience to this stage, you know, as a fact, that your body has a sexual energy centre located in your groin, and that your organism is keenly aware of the unrefined, hard to control, all-consuming nature of this energy. Now you are ready to begin the natural process of refining and transmuting this raw energy. You will learn either to raise this energy or to release it, usually via orgasm: for what seems the longest time, you will probably utilise both practices.

Before you begin the practice of raising and transmuting your body's naturally produced sexual energy, it will be helpful if you have some understanding of how your psycho-physiological organism is constructed to accommodate and assist this process. Be clear: you have no need to understand the mechanics of this process to achieve success in transmuting sexual energy. Your heart lasts a lifetime, whether you understand its functioning or not.

The sexual energy, raised, purified and transmuted naturally, flows round your body in a continuous circular motion, powered by each inhalation and exhalation of breath. With the in-breath, the energy rises from the sexual energy centre, physically moves up the spine to the back of the brain, then moves to the crown of the head. With the out-breath, the energy passes to the front of the brain, down through the tongue which is touching the roof of the mouth, and down through the chest, accumulating in a swirling motion in the abdomen before returning to the sexual centre.

This cyclic flow of energy occurs naturally and spontaneously as you develop in this meditation. In time, with diligent daily practice, the energy will flow entirely automatically, requiring no effort on your part. This is a very good sign: be satisfied with your progress, not pleased with yourself.

In the practices of the Taoist esoteric yoga, Tibetan Buddhist yoga and Hindu Kuṇḍalinī yoga can be found very detailed and precise techniques to achieve this circulation of energy. These yogas are the product of very sophisticated, highly developed, implicate technologies. From the perspective of our Western cultures, based on the Judeo-Christian code of ethics and lacking broad-based spiritual depths, these yogas require specialised cultural terms which make them generally inaccessible to our spiritually under-developed Western societies.

This meditation, in fact this whole book, is an attempt to articulate the first steps in the process of integrating oneself fully into reality, in terms accessible to an ordinary, intelligent, Western person. What is taught here is a yoga as valid as its Eastern counterparts. It is expressed in a simple direct way because, spiritually speaking, we in the West are at a post-primitive and pre-civilised stage of cultural development.

Begin, then, the second step of the meditation on sexual energy. This involves a focussing of your awareness. This is simple to explain but hard for you to realise. Once you have gained the experience and skills to realise this step of the meditation, the natural functioning of your organism will spontaneously take over, and the energy will circulate, without any effort on your part, in a harmonious manner.

The practice required to raise the sexual energy, to power your own internal dynamic forces is simple. During the deep, slow in-breath, visualise the energy travelling from your groin, up your spine, to the very top, the crown, of your skull. During the deep, slow out-breath, visualise the energy travelling down from the crown, through the roof of your mouth, which your tongue is touching, down the front of the chest, through the abdomen, and back to the groin.

At the beginning of this practice the energy will most likely move in your imagination only. But as your skill develops with unwavering determination, you will, in time, experience the actual movement of this energy. Be assured that this is fact, not theory or fantasy.

If it helps you in the early stages, focus your awareness on an image of erotic significance to you, and in your imagination visualise this image located at the crown of your head. This is an aid which should be discarded once you have learned to raise your sexual energy. To be successful in your quest for enlightenment, you must face reality directly, not through your fantasies.

Once the energy begins to circulate naturally, spontaneously and effortlessly, the tensions in your organism will begin to resolve themselves. Your power and understanding will grow, as the circulating energy is transmuted into a clearer and clearer understanding of the nature and purpose of reality. Without succeeding in this practice, you cannot attain the final stage of enlightenment: success is available to you, regardless of the conditions of your life, provided you <u>Act</u> and meditate with unwavering determination.

. . . .

VI

The all-pervasive influence of the emotions

What is the all-pervasive influence of the emotions?

Every situation you experience can be analysed and understood as a specific arrangement of the ten conditions. The goal of the process of enlightenment is to free you, progressively, from the constraints of the ten conditions. The first stage of enlightenment gives you the capacity to sustain freedom from emotional and intellectual limitations.

This teaching emphasises the crucial importance of breaking free from the emotional constraints of your personality. Until you do this, you cannot begin to see the world as it is. As long as you operate within the emotional conditions of your personality you will have a distorted view of reality.

Prior to the first stage of enlightenment, one seeks satisfaction of emotional needs and desires; afterwards, emotional satisfaction is not such a priority. Before the first enlightenment, one's view of the world is coloured by one's own attitudes; afterwards, you see that the emotional difficulties you experienced were primarily caused by your own emotions, by yourself and none other. Before the first stage of enlightenment, you are driven to attain emotional satisfaction and fulfilment; afterwards, you learn to deal with your life freely and spontaneously.

Through your emotional projections, a process you only gradually become aware of, you create the specific aspects of reality which you experience. The purpose of this period of your life is to test your capacity to recognise, and break free from, your unconscious emotional projections. These tests are karmic in nature, and are designed to establish the extent to which you are detached from your emotions, the extent to which you understand your own nature.

Remember, reality can be understood as a unified, organic machine, and each of us is an essential component. Part of the functioning of the process is a constant testing of your capacity to remain detached and clear. By becoming detached from your deep-seated emotional responses, you will attain the psychological stage of enlightenment.

. . . .

How does one experience karmic testing?

Throughout your life, you feel in turn joy and sorrow, and move up and down, endlessly up and down. In a vain effort to smooth out this process, some try to control others; some try to control themselves; and some try to endure the highs and lows. This constant experiencing of opposites, life's highs and lows, is a natural process; enlightenment offers the only real escape from this endless play of opposites in your life.

When you are far removed from the psychological stage of enlightenment, the alternation of joys and sorrows occurs as a long-term pattern flowing throughout your life. As you get closer to the first enlightenment, this alternating of joy and sorrow becomes more and more rapid. A person close to this stage of enlightenment experiences a profound lack of stability in both inner and outer emotional conditions.

It is important to distinguish between such emotional transformations leading to the unfolding of awareness, and the constant transformation in conditions experienced by the emotionally immature. The difference lies in developing your capacity to endure and persevere through time. One who is moving towards enlightenment understands the instability of conditions as a learning process; one who is emotionally immature simply desires to experience positive rather than negative emotional conditions.

The degree to which your emotions alternate between the opposites of joy and sorrow is a function of karma. The specific circumstances and conditions of your life are formed and structured, by karma, to test your capacity to become free from attachments to joys and sorrows. Learn to become responsive to the direction of karma in your life; trust in your karma to guide you through the maze of joys and sorrows.

The commonest response to the difficulties experienced during intense periods of karmic testing is: why me? The answer is: there is a lesson you have to learn before you can progress in your inner development, before you can progress along the path we each must travel, and your current situation is specifically configured, precisely drawn together, to enable you to understand and learn the lesson. Continue to meditate, **Live** and **Act** throughout your life, and the difficulties will be overcome.

Do not think, foolishly, that you can escape your karma. You cannot successfully swim against the flow of reality, because you are an integral component of the one reality. Remember, the implacable process that is reality will devour your personality and its products, at its own pace and in its own way - this is the root cause of your emotional suffering.

In the midst of your life conditions, blown here and there by karma, overwhelmed by difficulties and the illusion that they are permanent, your feelings may revolve around despair. Sustained despair can lead to the utterly false and illusory attempt to escape your problems through ending them by suicide. The only sure way out of the suffering experienced in all limiting emotional conditions is to cultivate detachment, yet to remain fully involved in your day-to-day life.

. . . .

How does one live a full emotional life, yet remain detached?

The detached attitude of mind which results from the successful application of these teachings is not to be confused with the male heterosexual insensitivity to emotional conditions which is such a common and inherently harmful product of our culture. Nor is it to be confused with that perversion of masculinity involving denial or suppression of emotions, either one's own or other people's. These forms of behaviour, which are by no means the sole province of the heterosexual male, are a failure to face reality and result in suffering caused by the accumulation of negative karma.

Be clear: after you have attained the first stage of enlightenment, you will still have the capacity to experience the full range of human emotions. What differs is that you will no longer be driven compulsively by your emotions. You will live and love both fully and freely, aware of the implications of the choices you make at each moment.

The heart of the matter is this: you must develop the ability to stand back from any situation you encounter through experience, to the extent that you understand your emotional response as being only one, relatively illusory, component of the conditions establishing that situation. In reality, the emotions experienced before the first stage of enlightenment are products of the personality and have only relative and illusory substance. After the psychological stage of enlightenment, you have the option to see through the illusion and to experience the emotions truly pervading all of reality.

To practise detachment, you need to resist the force of your emotions: use deep meditative breathing to calm you in emotionally stressful conditions. Learn to understand and experience difficult situations in a wider context which embraces both your point of view and the other person's. Learn to be detached: in reality, you may or may not get what you want in any particular situation - it truly does not matter. In either event, your life still goes on and the path unfolds, now, before you.

Use your meditation to develop your sensitivity to the full potential of each moment. Your emotional suffering is only real if you lack the capacity to detach yourself from it. Your emotional suffering will pass once you are centred in the midst of conditions.

. . . .

How does one become detached from fear and desire?

Fear and desire are deeply intertwined in our lives. What we desire most is often what we fear most. Fear is, in reality, the inverse of desire - "No! I don't want that."

Both fear and desire, experienced with intensity, can be very stressful on your whole organism, both mind and body. To become detached, you must free yourself from this stress, which invariably occurs on the path to the first enlightenment. The first and simplest technique is to enter into deep, slow meditative breathing - this will have a calming effect on your whole system.

There is also a second, more advanced, technique available to you. However, to develop in the practice of this second meditative skill you will require considerable faith. Not faith in anything particular, just faith. Faith, pure and unbounded, grows in you naturally and spontaneously as your awareness unfolds of your role in the process that is reality. Your faith grows with the realisation of the fruits of meditation. Committed daily practice in meditation inevitably produces these fruits.

As the results of your meditation unfold, a simple fact will become clear to you. You will come to understand this fact gradually, with the certain knowledge of experience. This fact is that you and reality are one and indistinguishable.

This fact, which is the ultimate truth of reality, is not at all apparent to common sense. Only gradually will you come to understand what it means. When, finally, after many trials, you know through experience what it means, then and only then will you have attained the final stage of enlightenment.

Through time and meditation on your experiences, you will come to understand that you and karma are indistinguishably one. That is to say, everything that happens to you is a function of who you are and what you think, feel and do. It will slowly dawn on you that everything which happens in your life is part of a meaningful and purposeful pattern.

In time, with this realisation comes freedom from bondage to fear and desire. All along the path to the final stage of enlightenment, you will still have the capacity to experience fear and desire. However, through meditation, you can free yourself from attachment to fear and desire.

This freedom from attachment comes from realising that everything that happens in your life, everything, without exception, has meaning and purpose. All fear is relatively illusory, because what is happening, or will happen, is structured to teach you a lesson about your own nature. All desire is relatively illusory, because the conditions of your life will supply you with all you truly need to understand your own nature, which is the true nature of reality.

As your work in meditation develops, and your practical experience expands, you will experience a growing capacity for fearlessness and desirelessness in the face of reality. Reality is not to be feared, because you and reality are one. Trust what happens, however fearful, with a calm acceptance of the reality of life and death. Reality is not to be desired, because you and reality are one. Accept what you receive from life and have no doubt that it will be sufficient.

Put simply, whatever is happening will happen as it occurs; avoid letting your fear and desire interfere with the course of events. To develop your capacity for fearlessness and desirelessness, <u>Live</u> and <u>Act</u> throughout your life. Think long and deeply on this.

. . . .

Why is it crucially important to become detached from your anger?

Anger is the single most corrosive emotion you can experience. Anger stems from thwarted desire. Anger results from what you want being at odds with what you experience.

Anger is deceptively dangerous because it is such a satisfying emotion, particularly if, from one's own point of view, one appears to be in the right. Anger consumes your energies, and, if sustained over long periods, can consume your health. When you act in anger, it feels fulfilling, satisfying and righteous - in reality, it is an activity through which you oppose the natural flow of reality, and the resulting penalties which may be imposed on you can be horrendous.

To act on the basis of your anger is to insist on what you want, in the face of reality. This is the antithesis of the clear setting of yourself face to face with reality. You cannot successfully impose your will on reality without incurring severe penalties: sustained anger leads to sustained ill-health; profound anger leads, in time, to profound penalties.

As with all Implicate Technology disciplines, the remedy to be applied is simple. Firstly, when you are angry, calm yourself with deep, slow, meditative breathing. Secondly, never, ever, under any circumstances or conditions, act on the basis of your anger - wait until you are calm and then decide on your action.

This is not to say that you must passively accept the conditions that caused your anger. If the conditions you experience are unfair or unjust, use the power discipline, as taught in chapter 3, to change your circumstances. Fight, and fight hard, against forces which oppress you; but do so in harmony with the inherent implicate laws.

Don't act while you experience anger in the circumstances of your domestic life. Always wait until you have regained calm. If your anger is prompted by another person's genuine selfishness, the opportunity to act will invariably arise again.

The danger you risk is quite clear. If you act under the influence of anger, you will incur karmic consequences of a severely negative nature, according to the severity and duration of your anger. If you act spontaneously, with a calm clear mind, you will be dealing with any situation in a karmically positive way.

. . . .

Why is it crucially important to forgive?

In your life it can happen that you are wronged - unfairly, unjustly and apparently without rhyme or reason. Your sense of injury, in such a situation, is acute and very often considerably justified. If your pain is deep, and your sense of having been wronged is considerable, you may feel it is impossible, indeed stupid, to forgive one who has so clearly and unjustly mistreated you.

Be clear: when such situations occur in your life, you are being tested by the process that is reality. The operator, structuring the situation to create your pain and sorrow, is the implacable law of karma. Whether you are able to forgive, or not, will significantly determine the shape of your life.

Christianity teaches the moral necessity for forgiveness. The supreme example of forgiveness, in our Western cultures, is set by Jesus accepting and forgiving the suffering of his crucifixion, so that the prophecies of his culture might be fulfilled, and primitive peoples raised to an ethically-based civilisation. The secular Implicate Technology teaching of the clear setting face to face with reality deals only with the mechanics of the process of forgiveness - the morality of each situation is dealt with by your responding positively to the promptings of your karma.

The mechanics of the process of forgiveness are simple. If you remain attached to your suffering, and are unable to forgive, you will continue to incur negative karma. If you forgive the person or persons who wronged you, you will be relieved from the weight and burden of your accumulated negative karma, according to the degree of your forgiveness.

If you refuse to forgive the wrongs done to you, you will remain bound to the pattern of pain and sorrow which has brought about such a significant opportunity in your life. If you refuse to forgive, you are reinforcing your commitment to unenlightened behaviour. Reality will so structure itself that the opportunities to forgive will continue until you learn the lesson - this means you will continue to suffer through the workings of your karma.

To commit an act of genuine forgiveness is to release yourself from bondage to a specific pattern of pain and sorrow in your life. To forgive is to confirm your commitment to enlightenment, to affirm your determination to act in accordance with the flow of reality. Now reality will so structure itself, because you have learnt an important lesson, that your life moves on to the next lesson. This does not mean the end of your pain and sorrow; it simply means an opportunity to move closer to enlightenment.

The act of forgiveness is simplicity itself. Words alone are not forgiveness. Reality is beyond mere words such as: "I forgive you". For the forgiveness to be a genuine release from the burden of accumulated negative karma, it must involve a sincere stepping away from attachment to your pain and sorrow. Mere words may fool other people; they can never fool karma. Within yourself, you must become committed to detachment from your suffering - only then does the genuine act of forgiveness take place.

The first step in the sincere act of forgiveness is to become detached from your negative emotional responses. Calm, slow, meditative breathing will help you to achieve this. Think about this teaching in the context of your own life, long and carefully.

The second step in the sincere act of forgiveness is to convey the fact that you have forgiven to the person or persons who have wronged you. This can be conveyed in simple words, when and if a suitable opportunity arises. What you have to say, according to circumstances, is some variation on this theme: "These things happen. I was hurt, but we can all learn from experience".

Do not, foolishly, believe that a genuine act of forgiveness will cause your pain to disappear rapidly, nor that your life will suddenly be filled with what you desire as a reward. The consequence of a sincere act of forgiveness is to release you from the burden of your accumulated negative karma. The true benefit you derive, freed from attachment to your pain and sorrow, is to be set clearly face to face with your experience of reality. In this way, you progress along the path to enlightenment.

. . . .

What is the Implicate Technology teaching on the act of unconditioned giving?

A true act of giving is a gift from yourself to another, devoid of ulterior motive. A gift which is given with the expectation of a specific response is a limited, conditioned gift. True giving requires no particular response and is meaningful and beneficial for you whether or not the gift is accepted by the recipient.

The attitude of mind in which you give is of crucial importance. The true act of giving involves a natural, spontaneous desire to enhance the life of the recipient. Give according to your own intuitive nature, without being influenced by thoughts of the consequences for yourself.

Give without any strings attached. An act of giving with an expectation of certain responses is only manipulation of others disguised as generosity. Such an act produces negative karma.

True giving is an act carried out purely for the sake of the recipient. Once the gift is truly given you retain no hold or rights over it. The positive or negative karmic consequences of your action will be determined by the interaction between yourself and the recipient.

The teachings contained in this book are given freely to you, with no conditions attached. Teachings which lead to enlightenment are beyond price, so only the insignificant cost of this book is involved. This gift, the teaching of the clear setting face to face with reality, the practice leading to the clear understanding of the meaning and purpose of your life, is offered to you to enrich your life.

What is given to you through this teaching is given freely. You are free to make of this gift whatever you are able to. You owe nothing to the Implicate Technology Centre for this gift.

A gift can be repaid in many, many ways. True giving requires no material recompense. The gift of these teachings is repaid in full, as your life is enriched and transformed through the practice of these teachings.

. . . .

VII

Advice on failure to attain the psychological stage of enlightenment

VIII

Conclusion - the far journey

BIBLIOGRAPHY

GLOSSARY

Synopsis Of Contents

This Is Everything

<u>Live</u>

Live the teachings,

> **live** the teachings.

<u>Act</u>

Act according to your intuition.

> Don't interfere.
> Just let things happen.

The formula for attaining **Enlightenment** is:

Throughout your life, <u>Live</u> and <u>Act</u>